104 Funny Va

MW00901274

Knock Knock

Jokes 4 kids

(The Joke Book for Kids Book 5)

By: **Ryan O Williams**
3rd Edition, Published By Ryan O Williams
Copyright 2014, Row Books

Knock, Knock!
Who's There?
Happy!
Happy? who?
Happy Valentine's DAY!

1. Knock, knock.
Who's there?
Olive.

Olive who?
Olive You so much?

2. Knock, knock.
Who's there?
Howard.
Howard who?
Howard you like a kiss?

3. Knock, knock.
Who's there?
Frank .
Frank who?
Frank You for my Valentine Gift?

4. Knock, knock.
Who's there?
Time.
Time who?
Time for me to fall in love?

5. Knock, knock.
Who's there?
Time.
Time who?
Time for my to give you a gift?

6. Knock, knock.
Who's there?
Put.
Put who?
(sing)Put your head on my shoulder Hold me in your
    arms...(Sing rest of the lyrics

7. Knock, knock.
Who's there?
Mary.
Mary who?
Mary me please?

8. Knock, knock.
Who's there?
Sherwood .
Sherwood   who?
Sherwood love to be your valentine?

9. Knock, knock.
Who's there?
Halibut.
Halibut who?
Halibut a kiss on the cheek?

10. Knock, knock.
Who's there?
Eyesore.
Eyesore who?
Eyesore do like you?

11. Knock, knock.
Who's there?
Value.
Value who?
Value be mine?

12. Knock Knock.
Who's there?
General Lee.
General Lee who?
General Lee I don't eat this much chocolate.

13. Knock Knock.
Who's there?
Sid.
Sid who?
Sid down I made this for you!
(give a card or treat)

14. Knock Knock.
Who's there?
Luke.
Luke who?
Luke at all the Valentine candy!

15. Knock Knock.
Who's there?
Anita.
Anita who?
Can I have Anita piece of chocolate!

16. Knock Knock.
Who's there?
Mike.
Mike who?
Mike I be your valentine.

17. Knock Knock.
Who's there?
Clothes.
Clothes who?
Clothes the door behind you its cold in February.

18. Knock Knock.
Who's there?
Arthur.
Arthur who?
Arthur any more chocolate hearts?

19. Knock Knock.
Who's there?
Use to.
Use to who?
Use to be my valentine?

20. Knock Knock.
Who's there?
Harry.
Harry who?
Harry up! give me a kiss!

21. Knock Knock.
Who's there?
Abbott.
Abbott who?
Abbott time for a new valentine partner?
(just kidding!)

22. Knock Knock.

Who's there?
Harry.
Harry who?
Harry up! Let's find some flowers.

23. Knock Knock.
Who's there?
Doughnut.
Doughnut who?
Doughnut eat too much candy!

24. Knock Knock.
Who's there?
Another.
Another who?
Another piece of my heart

25. Knock.
Who's there?
Emma.
Emma who?
Emma real anxious, for a new valentine gift!

26. Knock Knock.
Who's there?
Esther.
Esther who?
Esther any room in your heart for me?

27. Knock Knock.
Who's there?
Esther.
Esther who?
Esther going to be candy in this teddy bear?

26. Knock Knock.
Who's there?
Esther.
Esther who?
Esther any way? I can be your valentine!

28. Knock Knock.
Who's there?
Esther.
Esther who?
Esther any chocolate in that cardboard heart?

29. Knock Knock.
Who's there?
Love.
Love who?
Love me or live with it!

30. Knock Knock.
Who's there?
Like.
Like who?
Like I have a clue?

31. Knock Knock.
Who's there?
In with.
In with who?
In with the new, out with the old?

32. Knock Knock.
Who's there?

Alma.
Alma who?
Alma time for a valentine gift?

33. Knock Knock.
Who's there?
Flowers.
Flowers who?
Flowers! wow you shouldn't have, "No really."

34. Knock Knock.
Who's there?
Wanda.
Wanda who?
I Wanda new valentine?

35. Knock Knock.
Who's there?
Alva.
Alva who?
Alva another piece of candy please!

36. Knock Knock.
Who's there?
Xavier.
Xavier who?
Xavier the memories we have.

37. Knock Knock.
Who's there?
Tamara.
Tamara who?
Tamara we will have a friend!

38.Knock, knock.
Who's there?
Gladys.
Gladys who?
Gladys Valentine day. Aren't you?

39. Knock Knock.
Who's there?
Red?
Red Who?
Red velvet cake, taste great!

40. Knock Knock.
Who's there?
Norma Lee.
Norma Lee who?
Norma Lee I don't have a valentine!

41. Knock Knock.
Who's there?
Olive.
Olive who?
Olive these roses!

42. Knock Knock
Who's there !
The key!
The key who ?
The key to your heart!

43. Knock Knock.
Who's there?

Frank.
Frank who?
Frank you for being my best friend!

44. Knock Knock.
Who's there?
Anita.
Anita who?
Anita year! to share with you!

45. Knock Knock.
Who's there?
That's!
That's who?
That's a lot of cup cakes!

46. Knock Knock.
Who's there?
Your not.
Your not who?
Your not going to sing again! Are you?

47. Knock Knock.
Who's there?
Jimmy.
Jimmy who?
Jimmy a big kiss!

48. Knock Knock.
Who's there?
Happy.
Happy who?
Happy Valentines Day!

50. Knock Knock.
Who's there?
Someone.
Someone who?
Someone loves you so much!

51. Knock Knock.
Who's there?
A new.
A new who?

Today I made A new friend.

52.   Knock Knock.
Who's there?
Heaven.
Heaven who?
Heaven seen you since last Valentine!

53. Knock Knock.
Who's there?
No really .
No really who?
No really cupid is knocking on the door, to my heart

54. Knock Knock.
Who's there?
Quiet.
Quiet who?
Quiet down please, I'm about to propose.

55. Knock Knock.
Who's there?
Propose .
Propose who?
When are you going to propose, I'm not getting any younger?

56. Knock Knock.
Who's there?
Grandma.
Grandma who?
Grandma enjoyed many Valentine's!

57. Knock, Knock!
Who's There?
Atlas.
Atlas who?
Valentine's Day is here again!

58. Knock, Knock!
Who's There?
Justin!

Justin who?
Justin time i made you a gift.

60. Knock, Knock!
Who's There?
Claus!
Claus. who?
Claus I love you mom and dad!

61. Knock, Knock!
Who's There?
Oscar!
Oscar who?
Oscar her if, I can be her valentine!

62. Knock, Knock!
Who's There?
Out!
Out who?
Out with the old, in with the new!

63. Knock, Knock!
Who's There?
Invite!
Invite who?
You are invited, to my Valentine party!

64. Knock, Knock!
Who's There?
Oscar!
Oscar who?
Oscar him if I can be, his valentine!

65. Knock, Knock!
Who's There?
Where
Where who?
Where is gift it suppose to be here!

66. Knock, Knock!
Who's There?
Those
Those who?
Those are some very
nice flowers!

67. Knock, Knock!
    Who's There?
    Aww!
    Aww who?
  Aww, You Shouldn't Have! No really!

68.Knock, Knock!
    Who's There?
    Japans!
    Japans who?
    Japans if we get to eat more candy!

69.Knock, Knock!

Who's There?
Celebrate!
Celebrate who?
Celebrate this day by giving you a hug!

70. Knock, Knock!
Who's There?
A,E,I,O,U!
A,E,I,O,U who?
Don't forget the Y... I love you!

71. Knock, Knock!
Who's There?
You see!
You see who?
You see that bright star, I named it after you!

72. Knock, Knock!
Who's There?
Ken!
Ken who?
Ken you open the door, You invited us!

73. Knock, Knock!
    Who's There?
    Joanna!
    Joanna who?
    Joanna another Valentine joke!

74. Knock, Knock!
    Who's There?
    Namath!
    Namath who?
    Namath I forgot to put on your card!

75. Knock, Knock!
Who's there?
Armageddon!
Armageddon who?
Armageddon another
Valentine day card!

76.Knock, Knock!
Who's There?
Juanita!
Juanita who?
Juanita go find a new Valentine!

77.Knock, Knock!
Who's There?
Juicy!
Juicy who?
Juicy see what I see! Another box of chocolate.

78.Knock, Knock!
Who's There?
Alaska!
Alaska who?
Alaska her for you!

79.Knock, Knock!
Who's There?

Aldo!
Aldo who?
Aldo anything for you!

80. Knock, Knock!
    Who's There?
    Alex!
    Alex who?
    Alex my mother if she can be your Valentine!

81. Knock, Knock!
    Who's There?
    Esther!
    Esther who?
    Esther any red velvet cake left!

82. Knock, Knock!
    Who's There?
    Alli!
    Alli who?
    Guess Alli knock on another door!

83. Knock, Knock!
    Who's There?
    Alli!
    Alli who?
    Alli sees you next Valentine's Day!

84. Knock, Knock!
    Who's There?
    Space!
    Space who?
    More space in heart for you!

85. Knock, Knock!
    Who's There?
    Anthony!
    Anthony who?
    Anthony you want me to add to do this Valentine card.

86. Knock, Knock!
    Who's There?
    Fonda!
    Fonda who?
    I'm very Fonda of you!

87. Knock, Knock!
    Who's There?
    That's!
    That's who?
    That's so very kind of you!

88. Knock, Knock!
    Who's There?
    Butter!
    Butter who?
    Butter not miss next valentine. DAD!

89. Knock, Knock!

Who's There?
Cereal!
Cereal who?
Cereal pleasure to enjoy this day with my family!

90.Knock, Knock!
    Who's There?
    Winner!
    Winner who?
    Winner we going to eat all this candy!

91.Knock, Knock!
    Who's There?
    Honey bee.
    Honey bee who?
    Honey bee a dear and be my Valentine!

92.Knock, Knock!

Who's There?
Trying !
Trying who?
Trying to get you to open your heart!

93.Knock, Knock!
   Who's There?
   What!
   What who?
   What chocolate cake again!

94.Knock, Knock!
   Who's There?
   Dozen!
   Dozen who?
   Dozen you party, every Valentine's Day!

95.Knock, Knock!
   Who's There?
   Jamaica!
   Jamaica who?
   Jamaica cake for me too!

96. Knock, Knock!
    Who's There?
    Probably!
    Probably who?
I'll probably do my homework after I eat all this candy!

97. Knock, Knock!
    Who's There?
    Boogie !
    Boogie who?
    Boogie down lets dance!

98. Knock, Knock!
    Who's There?
    Abbott!
    Abbott who?
    Abbott time to give you a hug!

99.Knock, Knock!
   Who's There?
   Avery !
   Avery who?
   Avery body needs a hug! Happy Valentine's Day.

100.Knock, Knock!
   Who's There?
   Time!
   Time who?
   Time to start your bonus Knock knock Jokes, In books 1
   to 4!

BONUS CONTENT
Plus + 25 form: 104 Knock Knock Jokes Book 1
Plus + 25 form: 104 Thanksgiving Knock Knock Jokes Book 2

New Years BOOK 4

1. Knock, knock.

Who's there?
Time.
Time who?
Time to get to Time Sqaure in New York?

2. Knock, knock.
Who's there?
Lettuse.
Lettuse who?
Lettuse enjoy the New year!

3. Knock, knock!
Who's there?
Lettuse.
Lettuse who?
Please Lettuse stay up late

4. Knock, knock.
Who's there?
Gladys.
Gladys who?
I'm Gladys this year is over?

5. Knock, knock.

Who's there?
Getting.
Getting who?
Getting ready for some fireworks?

6. Knock Knock.
Who's there?
Balloon.
Balloon who?
Quick grab a Balloon! There getting away

7. Knock Knock.
Who's there?
Gladys.
Gladys who?
Gladys a New Year! Arer't you?

8. Knock Knock.
Who's there?
Olive.
Olive who?
Olive watching the News Years Day parade!

9. Knock Knock.
Who's there?
Ho ho ho.
Ho ho ho who?
Sorry Santa your late!

10. Knock Knock.
Who's there?
Jack frost.
Jack frost who?
Ah! you know! the guy who made all this snow?

11. Knock Knock.
Who's there?
Five.
Five who?
Five, four, three, two, one Happy New Year!

12. Knock Knock.
Who's there?

General Lee.
General Lee who?
General Lee I don't stay up this late.

13. Knock Knock.
Who's there?
Sid.
Sid who?
Sid down. It's time to watch the ball drop!

14. Knock Knock.
Who's there?
Luke.
Luke who?
Luke at all the fireworks!

15. Knock Knock.
Who's there?
Anita.
Anita who?
Can I have Anita 15 minutes.(To stay up late)

16. Knock Knock.
Who's there?
Mike.
Mike who?
Mike I have more time?(To stay up late)

17. Knock Knock.
Who's there?
Clothes.
Clothes who?
Clothes the door behind you its cold outside.

18. Knock Knock.
Who's there?
Arthur.
Arthur who?
Arthur any more fireworks?

19. Knock Knock.
Who's there?
Use to.
Use to who?

Use to say that last New Years?

20. Knock Knock.
Who's there?
Harry.
Harry who?
Harry up! It's almost a new year!

21. Knock Knock.
Who's there?
Abbott.
Abbott who?
Abbott time for more a new year?

22. Knock Knock.
Who's there?
Harry.
Harry who?
Harry up! Let's find a good seat at the parade.

23. Knock Knock.
Who's there?
Doughnut.
Doughnut who?
Doughnut stay up to late!

24. Knock Knock.
Who's there?
Hosanna.
Hosanna who?
Hosanna going to be on a new years day float?Chrismas is
    over.(How's Santa)

25. Knock.
Who's there?
Emma.
Emma who?
Emma real anxious, for a new years day count down!

Thanks for reading, if like this book Please review on Amazon,

1. Knock, knock.
Who's there?
Dewey.
Dewey who?
Dewey have to wait so long to eat?

2. Knock, knock.
Who's there?
Harry.
Harry who?
Harry up, and cut the turkey!

3. Knock, knock!
Who's there?
Arthur.
Arthur who?
Arthur any punkin
pie left overs?

4. Knock, knock.
Who's there?
Gladys.
Gladys who?
Gladys
Thanksgiving.
I'm hungry?

5. Knock, knock.
Who's there?
Waddle.
Waddle who?
Waddle open the door the family is here?

6. Knock Knock.
Who's there?
Norma Lee.
Norma Lee who?
Norma Lee I don't eat this much!

7. Knock Knock.
Who's there?
Gladys.
Gladys who?
Gladys Thanksgiving! lets eat?

8. Knock Knock.
Who's there?

Olive.
Olive who?
Olive the sweet potato pie too!

9. Knock Knock.
Who's there?
Aida.
Aida who?
Aida lot more than I should have!

10. Knock Knock.
Who's there?
Dewey.
Dewey who?
Dewey have to wait for everyone else?

11. Knock Knock.
Who's there?
Diana.
Diana who?
Diana thirst too!

12. Knock Knock.
Who's there?
General Lee.
General Lee who?
General Lee I don't wait to eat !

13. Knock Knock.
Who's there?

Sid.
Sid who?
Sid down. It's time to eat!

14. Knock Knock.
Who's there?
Luke.
Luke who?
Luke at all the food!

15. Knock Knock.
Who's there?
Anita.
Anita who?
Anita plate please.

16. Knock Knock.
Who's there?
Mike.
mike who?
Mike you having more cranberry sauce?

17. Knock Knock.
Who's there?
Don.
Don who?
Don eat all the turkey, I want some more!

18. Knock Knock.
Who's there?

Arthur.
Arthur who?
Arthur any more sweet potatoes?

19. Knock Knock.
Who's there?
Wilma.
Wilma who?
Wil Ma make food or order out?

20. Knock Knock.
Who's there?
Harry.
Harry who?
Harry up! the food is burning!

21. Knock Knock.
Who's there?
Abbott.
Abbott who?
Abbott time for dessert isn't it?

22. Knock Knock.
Who's there?
Odette.
Odette who?
Odette's a big punkin pie!

23. Knock Knock.
Who's there?

Phillip.
Phillip who?
Phillip your plates and dig in!

24. Knock Knock.
Who's there?
Phyllis.
Phyllis who?
Phyllis my plate up too!

25. Knock.
Who's there?
Emma.
Emma who?
Emma real hungry!

Thanks for reading, if like this book Please review on Amazon

Have a Merry Christmas and Happy New Year: Ryan O William

Bonus From: Book 1
104 Knock knock jokes
on Kindle Amazon:

By: Ryan O Williams

http://www.amazon.com/dp/B00GWUO83M

1. Knock, knock.
Who's there?
Dewey.
Dewey who?
Dewey have to wait so long to eat?

2. Knock, knock.
Who's there?
Harry.
Harry who?
Harry up, and cut the turkey!

3. Knock, knock!
Who's there?
Arthur.
Arthur who?
Arthur any punkin
pie left overs?

4. Knock, knock.
Who's there?
Gladys.
Gladys who?
Gladys
Thanksgiving.
I'm hungry?

5. Knock, knock.
Who's there?
Waddle.
Waddle who?
Waddle open the door the family is here?

6. Knock Knock.
Who's there?
Norma Lee.
Norma Lee who?
Norma Lee I don't eat this much!

7. Knock Knock.
Who's there?
Gladys.
Gladys who?
Gladys Thanksgiving! lets eat?

8. Knock Knock.
Who's there?
Olive.

Olive who?
Olive the sweet potato pie too!

9. Knock Knock.
Who's there?
Aida.
Aida who?
Aida lot more than I should have!

10. Knock Knock.
Who's there?
Dewey.
Dewey who?
Dewey have to wait for everyone else?

11. Knock Knock.
Who's there?
Diana.
Diana who?
Diana thirst too!

12. Knock Knock.
Who's there?
General Lee.
General Lee who?
General Lee I don't wait to eat !

13. Knock Knock.
Who's there?
Sid.

Sid who?
Sid down. It's time to eat!

14. Knock Knock.
Who's there?
Luke.
Luke who?
Luke at all the food!

15. Knock Knock.
Who's there?
Anita.
Anita who?
Anita plate please.

16. Knock Knock.
Who's there?
Mike.
mike who?
Mike you having more cranberry sauce?

17. Knock Knock.
Who's there?
Don.
Don who?
Don eat all the turkey, I want some more!

18. Knock Knock.
Who's there?
Arthur.

Arthur who?
Arthur any more sweet potatoes?

19. Knock Knock.
Who's there?
Wilma.
Wilma who?
Wil Ma make food or order out?

20. Knock Knock.
Who's there?
Harry.
Harry who?
Harry up! the food is burning!

21. Knock Knock.
Who's there?
Abbott.
Abbott who?
Abbott time for dessert isn't it?

22. Knock Knock.
Who's there?
Odette.
Odette who?
Odette's a big punkin pie!

23. Knock Knock.
Who's there?
Phillip.

Phillip who?
Phillip your plates and dig in!

24. Knock Knock.
Who's there?
Phyllis.
Phyllis who?
Phyllis my plate up too!

25.   Knock.
Who's there?
Emma.
Emma who?
Emma real hungry!

1. Knock, Knock!
Who's There?
Old man!
Old man who?
He's an old man, cause he had a candy cane!

2. Knock, Knock!
Who's There?
That guy
That guy who?
That guy at the mall, is not the real Santa is he!

3. Knock, Knock!
Who's There?
Those
Those who?
Those are some very
tall elves at the mall!

4. Knock, Knock!
    Who's There?
    Aww!
    Aww who?
  Aww, You Shouldn't Have! No really!

5.Knock, Knock!
    Who's There?
    Japans!
    Japans who?
    Japans what we are getting for Christmas!

6.Knock, Knock!
    Who's There?
    Jerome!
    Jerome who?
    Does Santa Jerome around the north pole!

7.Knock, Knock!

Who's There?

Peanut!

Peanut who?

No Peanut butter and jelly today!

8.Knock, Knock!

Who's There?

You see!

You see who?

You see that snowflake falling down!

9.Knock, Knock!

Who's There?

Ken!

Ken who?

Ken you open the door, You invited us!

10.Knock, Knock!
Who's There?
Joanna!
Joanna who?
Joanna another knock knock joke!

11.Knock, Knock!
Who's There?
Namath!
Namath who?
Namath your name first!

12.Knock, Knock!
Who's there?
Armageddon!
Armageddon who?
Armageddon another gift!

13.Knock, Knock!
Who's There?
Juanita!
Juanita who?
Juanita another cookie!

14.Knock, Knock!
Who's There?
Juicy!
Juicy who?
Juicy see what I see! A sled on the roof.

15.Knock, Knock!
Who's There?
Alaska!
Alaska who?
Alaska Santa for a new bike!

16.Knock, Knock!
Who's There?
Aldo!

Aldo who?
Aldo anything for video game system!

17.Knock, Knock!
  Who's There?
  Alex!
  Alex who?
  I'll Alex Santa the questions if you don't mind!

18.Knock, Knock!
  Who's There?
  Esther!
  Esther who?
  Esther you're the real Santa or not!

Book 2
104 Thankgiving Knock knock jokes
on Kindle Amazon:
By: Ryan O Williams

http://www.amazon.com/dp/B00GSZK6QO

Book 3
104 Christmas Knock knock jokes
on Kindle Amazon:
By: Ryan O Williams
http://www.amazon.com/dp/B00GWUO83M

Book 4
104 New Year's Knock knock jokes
on Kindle Amazon:
By: Ryan O Williams
http://www.amazon.com/dp/B00H25PZMO

60467487R00033

Made in the USA
Lexington, KY
07 February 2017